NEW ZEALAND
LAND
AND
PEOPLE

CRAIG POTTON

INTRODUCTION BY
DAVID YOUNG

CRAIG
POTTON
PUBLISHING

Photographs: Craig Potton.
Text: David Young.
Printing: Astra Print Ltd, Wellington.

Published by Craig Potton Publishing, Box 555, Nelson, New Zealand.
©1999 Craig Potton Publishing

ISBN 0 908802 49 8

NEW ZEALAND

Ninety Mile
Beach

● Whangarei

TASMAN SEA

AUCKLAND ●

Bay of Plenty

Hamilton ● ● Tauranga   East Cape

● Rotorua

● Taupo   ● Gisborne

Lake Taupo

Rūapehu   Hawkes Bay
2797m   ● Napier

Mt Taranaki
2518m

● Wanganui

Golden Bay   ● Palmerston North

Nelson ●   ● Masterton

● Westport   WELLINGTON ●

● Kaikoura

Hokitika ●

SOUTH PACIFIC
OCEAN

Franz Josef ●   Mt Cook
3754m   ● CHRISTCHURCH

Mt Aspiring
3027m

Milford Sound   ● Timaru

Queenstown ● Lake Wakatipu   ● Oamaru

Lake Te Anau
Lake Manapouri

● DUNEDIN

● Invercargill

Stewart Island

INTRODUCTION

Raetihi, Central North Island

Though I love my country, I have recently been troubled by a daydream. Consider a perfect New Zealand beach, rippled dunes and a pinafore of clean sand spilling down between two rocky headlands towards a single wave breaking on the shoreline. A group of locals stand on the shore looking out to sea. With rising anticipation they watch as a corked bottle surfaces on the incoming breakers. When the bottle beaches, they fall upon it, break it open and solemnly read the message contained inside. Some then race off to forcefully impose its cryptic demands on everyone else around the country: 'Forget about how we did things before,' they insist. 'This new message is how we are doing them now.'

I think the image arises from a tension within the culture in this land. The paradox is that while we seem to be wide open to new ideas, in another sense we never let go of old ones. Outward-looking, innovative and ready for change, New Zealanders are open to adopting ideas haphaz-ardly, even if they strain our somewhat fragile traditions. Being ready to change can be a virtue, giving us the opportunity to overcome negative habits. However, New Zealand is also a place where these new ideas can quickly become steel-trap orthodoxies, seized upon and enforced with uncritical and fierce conformity. It seems not to matter that their imposi-tion might diminish people's lives. One might feel that this is the behav-iour of a society with scant regard for its collective memory, and little respect for its past. Indeed, these could be the symptoms of a society in a degree of crisis: is this how a small, recently colonised group of islands deals with the issue of cultural identity in the era of Americanisation and globalisation?

During the first contact with Europeans, Maori society proved itself to be startlingly agile and adaptable. We know that Maori were not only adept traders, but that they also seized on expensive technology such as flour mills with an alacrity that almost equalled the willingness of their English village counterparts to industrialise agriculture. Mill remnants from these early ventures may still be found in many parts of the North Island, particularly in the King Country and Bay of Plenty.

Until the New Zealand Wars, Maori tribes also purchased and operated their own trading craft, the better to capitalise on the markets they, as tribes, had developed to food-hungry towns such as Auckland. Furthermore, by the mid 1800s there were more literate Maori than there were Pakeha (New Zealanders of European descent). In part, Maori literacy was an expression of their willingness to embrace the teachings of Christian missionaries. Yet it has to be said that Maori society also clings to ideas that may be well past their 'shelf life'. The most visible of these is its widespread refusal to allow women speaking rights on marae, even new marae such as those at Victoria University or our new national museum, Te Papa.

As a nation then, New Zealanders, Maori and Pakeha alike, take to both technology and new ideas like ducks to water. Sometimes this is highly beneficial. Inspired by the far-sighted vision of Yellowstone National Park in the USA, we picked up and ran with the idea, creating the fourth national park in the world in 1887. We were also, in 1893, the first nation in the world to give votes to women. With the progressive Liberals, we were first on the shop floor with innovative and compassionate industrial relations legislation in 1894. In fitful ways, the innovation has continued. We were to the forefront of developing a welfare state in the 1930s, and leading liberation movements such as anti-apartheid and nuclear-free. Following the huge success of campaigns for the belated protection of native forests, in 1991 Parliament passed into law the comprehensive Resource Management Act, with its integrating principles promoting sustainable development. Such openness to change has created one of the most legislating, reforming parliaments in the world, with all the advantages and disadvantages that that entails.

This open approach to new ideas and experimentation (along with good soil and climate) also makes for one of the planet's most productive agricultural systems – second to none when it comes to dairying and forestry production. Hand-in-glove with this we have also displayed a reckless willingness to dispense several generations of newfangled chemical sprays, from DDT to PCP, to the detriment of both consumers and agricultural and timber workers. An estimated 4,000 tonnes of active pesticide ingredients are still spread in New Zealand every year, not counting the extensive use of pest poisons on farmland and native forests.

We are also about as computer-equipped, computer-literate and Internet-linked as anyone else in the world. Stories continue to surface of Kiwi go-getters who can make fortunes by producing a software fix for the Y2K (Year 2000) computer glitch. There are local software companies who 'hotdog' commercially onto the Internet, or develop startling computer graphics, like home-grown Taylormade. This Dunedin company burst onto world television screens with its America's Cup graphics. Its inspiring and continuing story is an electronic refashioning of the cherished myth of the practical Kiwi who can do anything with a bit of No. 8 fencing wire.

Perhaps our national tendencies stem from the fact that those who emigrated to this country travelled in search of Utopia. They abandoned the problems of the Old World but inevitably failed to find what they came for in the New. So it was that they turned to a mild version of what anthropologists call 'cargo cultures' from other nations to satisfy their dreams. Even today, once the cargo is here, we never let go of it. Perhaps this thesis may partly explain why we used to have a dogged ability to keep old cars on the road long after they had disappeared into scrap metal everywhere else except the third world. More recently we have shucked off that reputation of austere self-sufficiency, exchanging it for what is really its opposite. Now we have cheap car imports from Japan and a collateral persistent balance of payments problem.

But there are numerous examples of ideas – elsewhere trapped like beetles in museum amber – still creeping about our sand dunes. My favourite example, from a visiting academic Lyman Sargeant, is that of the Golden Dawn, a Theosophical Society movement founded in Fabian England in the 1890s. With a few exceptions, such as southern California, the Golden Dawn faded from the countries in which it was founded early this century. A single chapter of it marched bravely on in Havelock North until 1974!

Other more mainstream ideologies and movements have struck fertile soil here. Feminism caught on in New Zealand as it never did in Europe or the United States, though it may now be under stress. Like socialism, anti-racism and other liberating 'isms' of the 1960s, after 30 years it shows serious signs of being displaced by another international trend, the narcissism of the youth sub-culture, and the irresistible cult of consumerism.

Even if they arrived in abandoned magnums, until the 1960s, such internationally-inspired distractions seldom seemed to breach the essential fabric of society. New Zealanders were, and still are, perceived as

Heretaniwha Point and Ohinemaka Beach, South Westland

friendly, even though writer Bruce Lyons argues with some point that this is essentially a strategy devised by a people who dislike open conflict. We perpetuated the myth that this was a great place to bring up children – and many of us lived the truth of that. Nothwithstanding a welter of shaming statistics on that subject today, potentially it still is such a place.

A generation ago we were a people whose ties with agriculture were close. Even among urban people, a large proportion had come off farms or retained close links with farming. That is no longer true, and perhaps the loss of that agricultural base has undermined some of the social values that once contributed to more likeable aspects of the so-called Kiwi character. I recently heard a drought and fire-afflicted Central Otago farmer on the radio. In making a case for some sort of Government support for the plight of his people, he added the poignantly quaint phrase, 'just quietly'. Those words of understated pleading seemed to echo a gentler time, when brash public relations campaigning and orchestrated one-upmanship was not so prevalent. To me those words speak of a people who, with their feet firmly on the ground, once knew the difference between straight-talking and manufactured hype.

The big changes occurred in the 1980s. Under Roger Douglas, who was the Minister of Finance in the 'new right' Labour Government elected in 1984, the nation was compelled to drink deeply from a trough labelled 'monetarism'. This had drifted across the Pacific from the USA, where it was called 'Reaganomics'. Today it is abundantly clear that the gap between rich and poor has grown tremendously. In an effort to reduce government debt, and to increase efficiencies, the family silver, as they say, has all been sold, including the state owned telecommunication company, the railways, and electricity generation; the kinds of assets that few nations sell off. Though other western countries have also sold off Government assets, few have pursued this policy with the vigour of New Zealand. Sadly, now, with significant segments of society laid waste, the nation is economically no better off than it was before and socially far worse off.

However, while the New Zealand version of monetarism has had this downside, there is no doubt that the radical recreation that is post-1984 New Zealand is a society less regulated, apparently freer. People like myself, self-employed, with their mortgages largely paid and their children essentially educated, enjoy freedom of choice and freedom of movement and work-styles, that are unsurpassed anywhere. Our access to the flowering of our literature, music and visual arts; to the benefits of our increasingly multi-cultural society; to a burgeoning cafe society; and to an

amazing environment and astonishing recreational opportunities is a great blessing. There is also the excitement of living in a society still in the making, largely uninhibited by the weight of the past. However, the dreams of my generation and those before us of a liberal democracy that upholds ideas of social justice and equal opportunity, today seem far away indeed.

Under the doctrine of monetarism, most of us have come to be more than willing to take greater responsibility for our actions. But the manic force of continuing policies means that New Zealanders are not quite the relaxed people they were a generation ago. Even the middle income earners are anxious about the great passages of life for themselves and their families. It has not been like this since the Great Depression, whose blight was eased by the first Labour Government. In return for less government, less tax and diminishing social justice, we are supposed to have more choices. But this is true only for those who can pay – for many, choice is simply an illusion. For example, health and education, in spite of increased spending, are, more than ever before, catspaws of ideologies. Consequently, the lives of workers in these sectors are made increasingly difficult and private alternatives made to look increasingly attractive. Yet because the World Bank dream is not one that most New Zealanders have ever shared, or ever sought, cynicism about politics has broken out at levels I believe are dangerous for democracy. All the opinion polls, and the diminishing number of citizens who turn out to vote on polling day, provide evidence of this cynicism.

Perhaps the greatest sacrifice since the 1980s has been trust. Whether between politicians and constituents, employee and employer, rich and poor, so much of that vital glue has been lost. Loyalty, even to country, has been another casualty. Who can blame young people, slogged by the interest rates on student loans and often without hope of constructive work here, for heading overseas? It is hardly surprising that, for a range of reasons, educated young people are becoming one of our largest exports. While there are no easy solutions to this problem, the society without a memory could become the society without a future.

While as a culture we seem to accept outside influences with open arms, and adapt readily to new international trends, there is a huge irony that our natural history is exceptionally conservative, exhibiting the very reverse of our cultural traits. A long, island isolation that predates the advent of the mammals has led to a population of native animals and plants that has survived and evolved in unique ways in the 60–80 million years since New Zealand sheared off from the super-continent that was

Gondwana. These natural inhabitants 'keep the faith' of the DNA stock that once existed back on the mainland, but often is no more. Many of our icons, birds such as kiwi, takahe, and kakapo; reptiles such as tuatara; insects like weta; and the giant forest trees such as kahikatea and totara are ancient survivors that would never have endured in the more predatory world of the continental land masses.

The analogy, in human terms, might be the Book of Kells tended by Gaelic monks during Europe's long period of benightedness and invasions from the north. The illuminated text maintained the light of Christian scholarship in uniquely lovely forms at the extremes of western civilisation. The difference is that nature in isolation continues to evolve. That makes the native animals and ecosystems that live here unique, precious and special.

In looking for a way forward for New Zealand, it seems we should draw on what is distinctive and unique in our landscape, our stories and our music:

Smoko, shearing shed, Golden Bay

ourselves. Another strand of the fabric that makes this country special has to do with the presence of Maori. The richness of their language and culture, their waiata, poi and haka have for a century or so at least added a taniko border to the national cloak that most Pakeha felt comfortable about wearing. For a long time Maori cultural expression was limited to the ceremonial, confined to coins and stamps of the realm, or used to welcome visiting Royalty.

The founding document of New Zealand, the Treaty of Waitangi, was signed in 1840. It set down rights and obligations for both the new European settlers and the indigenous Maori tribes. Since the early 1980s the Treaty has actively been 'doing business', and Maori have attained prominence in ways some Pakeha have felt less comfortable with. Certainly, it is the strident Maori protesters, sometimes tattooed and dreadlocked, who attract most media attention. But Maori demands are for return of land and compensation for a multitude of other losses, physical and spiritual, inflicted by the colonists. These protests are founded upon a history of injustice, if not of strong legal precedent and justification.

Challenged though many New Zealanders may be by such demonstrations, this is but one strand of an important relationship. Over the past 30 years particularly, Maori have conferred a great gift of teaching on those other New Zealanders willing to listen to them. They have taught us not only to be respectful of Maori rights, tikanga and tradition, but have also shown glimpses of the riches afforded from living in a more fully bi-cultural society. There is also a raised sensitivity to issues of race and culture that often distinguishes us from many other post-colonials when we travel abroad. The main impediment to these developments has been the comfort zones of people who are challenged by the Maori renaissance.

Long-time critic of the Crown, Professor Ranginui Walker has, however, acknowledged the progress on Maori claims under the Treaty of Waitangi. Making this possible, he says, has been a Pakeha willingness to look at past history and concede that Maori had not previously been given 'a fair go'. So that tenet of our earlier society has not, after all, entirely disappeared. We are still some way yet from ideal race relations, but there is a sense of moving forward, particularly with the settlement of claims with some of the major tribes, such as Tainui and Ngai Tahu. If the Treaty settlements can be criticised for failing to reach those on the margins of Maori society, especially the urban proletariat, or for being inadequate, they have also created a climate in which a number of remarkable initiatives have taken place.

Some iwi authorities are now becoming responsibly engaged in the day-to-day care of their people. In what was the old police station at Opotiki, the Whakatohea tribe now run their own iwi health clinic. The doctor is tangata whenua, from the local iwi or tribe. Such self-help community models are increasingly used all over the country: iwi universities are now well-established in several parts of New Zealand. These also enable Maori to take responsibility for Maori language education at several levels. The initiatives offer refreshing alternatives to the downward-spiralling consequences of state welfare dependency. They may provide a model too for a decentralised society of distinct communities.

At the same time, Maori continue to have an influence on the rest of us. The way in which so many Pakeha funerals are conducted today is surely an example. The recent tradition of friends and family getting up to recall to assembled mourners the memory and humour of the lives of the deceased owes as much to exposure to Polynesian ceremony as it does to the decline of a patriarchal priesthood. The upsurge in certain types of tattooing as body ornament, too, may be connected to a growing multi-culturalism.

Concurrently, a number of other significant bi-cultural developments are taking place. They cannot all be discussed, so let me limit myself to some examples from the language, the arts and the land, all of which may be seen as critical to the model of an evolving, self-directing and fully democratic society.

Despite a media dominated by international culture and consumerism, attempts to safeguard and revive the Maori language doggedly continue. My local urban swimming pool, in the summer of 1999, has for the first time been assailed by vigorous learn-to-swim instruction in fluent Maori to classes of Maori children. It gives a whole new meaning to the term, 'Maori immersion classes'. Slowly, and in a variety of ways, the Maori language is fighting to become again a vibrant aspect of life in these islands. At the same time our law, particularly environmental law, is taking up Maori terms. While such indicators should not be over-esti-mated, they now are part of continuing trends that 30 years ago were unthinkable.

Another telling example is the phenomenon of Huia Publishers. Huia is a virtually all-Maori operation founded in 1991, with some 15 full-time employees today. It is thoroughly professional, and committed to the growth of Maori writing, language, history and culture. The Huia Short Story Awards ceremony leaves one marvelling at developments that even a decade ago would have seemed impossible. Here are several hundred people, mostly Maori, gathering in support of the writers and judges of the various sections. Maori language and talent are to the fore, and the best work produced is anthologised. One of Huia's star writers, Briar Grace-Smith has this year had her artful, moving and universal play *Purapurawhetu* published, to great acclaim.

While it is clear a distinct, bi-cultural society is being created here before our eyes, it will not be truly bi-cultural until a number of things change. Until Pakeha can be as comfortable moving between the two worlds as Maori have had to become. Until Maori mortality rates compare with those of other New Zealanders. Until Maori achieve in the education and employment stakes as well as their Pakeha counterparts. And perhaps this process will not be complete until Polynesian migrants from the islands of the South Pacific, the quiescent volcano in our society, begin to take a more equal place in our media, in local and national government and in business.

And lest I am accused of peddling ideas from notes in bottles myself, let me tell a story about a recent wedding I attended. This celebrated the marriage of the grandson of an old Maori friend, now deceased, from the Whanganui River. The friend had been a Maori activist most of his life. His daughter was the mother of twin boys, by an Indian. It was the wedding of one of the twins and he was marrying a Cambodian, daughter of refugees. The first part of the service was Buddhist, the second in a Catholic church. Their beautiful two year-old daughter looked equally at home with her Maori and Cambodian relatives. The wedding banquet was Cambodian, while official announcements were made by Maori backed by guitars and singing. The twin brother, who works in Scotland, attended the wedding resplendent in a genuine Scots kilt. These people reveal the kind of pathway that a number of our children will venture down. And they remind us that being Maori, or anything else, is at least as much about culture as it is about genes.

In an era of pluralism, though, where lies the common ground? Clearly, the Maori influence on Pakeha and vice versa, is at its most practical and, potentially, spiritual when it comes to valuing and protecting nature.

At the frontline in this challenge is the government run Department of Conservation (DOC), which controls around a third of New Zealand's land area. DOC has begun to enter into cooperative management with some iwi. It now has 13 agreements, nine with the South Island's Ngai Tahu settlement, covering such matters as recognition of the spiritual significance to Maori of Aoraki (Mt Cook) and the vesting of the Arahura Valley, a traditional source of greenstone, in the tribe.

Whatever has been given back by the Government seems small compared with the magnitude of what was originally taken (most of the South Island) for a pittance. Despite a succession of broken promises and the one-sided pattern of appropriation by the Government over 150 years, such agreements continue to involve much good faith. One that stands out in recent years is with another tribe, Ngati Koata, of the Marlborough Region, whose mana over the island of Takapou-rewa

Kakapo, Maud Island, Marlborough Sounds

(Stephens Island) was recently recognised by the Government. For its part, the tribe agreed to forgo its claim on the island under the Treaty, leaving the island as a nature reserve. The island's treasures include tuatara, rare native frogs and huge numbers of breeding seabirds.

To acknowledge these agreements is not to diminish the significance of the outstanding claims that remain. Settlement suggests, however, that cooperation is possible, as well as necessary. The next step is to find a way to bring Maori and Pakeha together under the Treaty in ways that recognise the covenant between them that is rooted in the land.

Now we have another opportunity to lift bi-cultural and community cooperation generally. This is the recently published draft of the New Zealand Biodiversity Strategy, part of the honouring of our commitment as a nation to the accord hammered out at the UNCED environment conference in Rio in 1992. This new document, designed to engage all New Zealanders – the public, non-government organisations and local government – points the way forward.

The document is significant for New Zealand for two reasons. First, this country has plants and animals that have evolved uniquely for the millions of years since we separated from Gondwana. According to internationally renowned ecologist Jarad Diamond, natural New Zealand can be described as the place on earth most akin to life on another planet. Make no mistake, this is a special land. Here, large flightless birds like the kiwi, kakapo and the now extinct moa evolved, filling the niches usually occupied by mammals. Giant weta stepped, antennae swaying, into the niche taken elsewhere by mice. But because of the introduction of mammalian predators, and a long legacy of habitat destruction by both Maori and European, those keystone species that have survived are in such low numbers that both birds and their habitat survive beneath a terrible question mark. Extinction of species has become a dismal phantom of our landscape, mainly because our unique flora and fauna have no mechanisms for dealing with invaders brought by both Maori and Pakeha. Thirty-two per cent of our indigenous land and freshwater birds are extinct. Twice that amount (63 per cent) of forest has been converted to farms, exotic forests, settlements and roads. Almost one third of our seabirds are extinct; three of the seven native frog species; one fish, one bat and possibly three reptile species. The status of one thousand of our known animal, plant and fungi species remains threatened. Most of what is protected is in uplands and mountains. Some of it is undergoing severe destruction by exotic predators, the most obvious being the Australian possum, whose prodigious capacity for reproduction is today barely held in check by strategic campaigns of poisoning.

But despite such a dismal picture, the wonderful thing about New Zealand conservationists is that they have not given up. Both government and voluntary conservation groups are stepping up their fight against introduced pests and weeds; regaining and restoring vital habitat; and working to increase bird populations.

The biodiversity strategy aims to do much more than simply conserve what remains. Ideally, like a number of government initiatives, it would serve to muster support at the level of urban communities, hapu (sub-tribes) and local government in order to enhance and sustain indigenous biodiversity.

Cities are great consumers of resources, not least of which are food, timber, gravel and hydro power. For city dwellers, doing their bit for the environment can amount to little more than separating the chardonnay bottles from the yoghurt pottles before putting out the rubbish. In fairness, this is a failure of opportunity, leadership and education. Most people want to do the right thing. For that reason it seems unfortunate that since 1995 developers and environmentalists have been unable to agree on a scheme for farming wind power off Wellington's beautiful, wind-bountiful coastlines. Environmentalists in the fuller sense of the term appreciate, I believe, that there are always trade-offs, but a good solution minimises environmental costs. The people of Palmerston North clearly felt quite differently about the very evident windmills on their skyline that will produce much of the power for their region.

Of course there remains a significant number of environmental activists with great vision and energy who are capable of harnessing urban dreamers. They range from the likes of Pureora tree-climbing protest veteran Stephen King through to the new generation of activists who are behind Native Forest Action, the group currently fighting native forest exploitation on the West Coast. Indeed sometimes the most productive of convergences occur when city dreams and city energies are combined with the needs of the rural landscape and its owners.

Much of New Zealand's ground-breaking environmental work has been achieved on offshore islands, where Government scientists have hauled a range of birds and plants back from the cliff of extinction. The most celebrated success has been Don Merton's work with the Chatham Island black robin on Little Mangere Island. As the world now knows, with one female robin and seven males left in the world, the Merton team was able to ensure the continued existence of that species, which is now well out of danger. Less publicised but equally significant is the recent extermination from Kapiti Island (which is an island of 2000 ha) of not just possums but, remarkably, rats. This has meant that for the purposes of nurturing an even wider number of animals and plants, this large island may now be regarded as free of exotic predators.

These islands, where some of the first significant gains for conservation were made, are now becoming an inspiration for recovery programmes on the mainland. Perhaps the most ambitious of these is at Karori Sanctuary, a former Wellington City water catchment reserve run by a trust that in 1999 built an 8.6 kilometre predator-proof fence. This will mean that within the city limits of the capital, visitors will be able to view a variety of birds, animals and plants that lived in the region prior to human settlement.

This will serve a number of purposes. It will encourage the breeding cycles of birds already there in small numbers, such as tui, grey warblers, fantails and pigeon. More dramatically, it is proposed that a variety of now rare animals, including weka, tuatara, kokako and two species of kiwi will be reintroduced. A range of gecko and lizards, Powelliphanta (native land snail) and long-tailed bats is also on the agenda, as are such threatened plants as mistletoe and rata.

The benefits will not end there. Those birds, such as tui, bellbird, kereru, kaka and others that will fly from the sanctuary, will also grace the suburbs north and south with their presence. In some instances, these suburbs are rapidly and naturally regreening, particularly on their higher slopes. Indeed, wherever open space and rainfall permit, usually on uneconomic farmland, New Zealand is undergoing botanical recovery. So given half a chance nature is doing its best to spread the seed and as it does so it 'spreads the word'.

DOC's official 'mainland island' recovery programme involves six sites totalling over 9,400 ha in all, including Hurunui in the South Island and Boundary Stream in the North. These sites are being heavily managed to reduce predators to create breeding sanctuaries for native flora and fauna. Another 15 projects, among them the highly successful Mapara project, near Te Kuiti and the possum fence that sequesters Cape Brett, are doing similar work but are not formally designated as 'islands'. It is only resource supply that limits this challenging and inspirational concept from growing more quickly.

However, for all the improvements taking place on land, our greatest struggle to protect what is special may lie in the marine environment. New Zealand is, in every sense – mythically, climatically, historically, psychologically and physically – a maritime nation. A possible 80 per cent of our country's total biodiversity is estimated to live in the sea. Yet less than one per cent of our maritime zone, the fourth largest in the world, has received any kind of scientific examination, let alone protection.

A belated, but now burgeoning response to the needs of the marine environment has been the development of fully protected, mostly coastal, marine reserves. The nation's first, at Leigh, between Auckland and Whangarei, is now almost 25 years old. Its 7 kilometre by 800 metre total protection zone has demonstrated the phenomenal capacity of all species, plant and fish, to replenish their numbers. In recent years 16 more have been created. Another 12 await approval, although entire coastlines, for instance from Akaroa south to the Nuggets in deep Southland, still languish without any form of protection.

The biodiversity strategy is vital, the more so given that environmentalism seems to be fading in the public mind as a cause. Support for all environmental movements has fallen dramatically since the beginning of this decade and with it, though not necessarily related, has come what seems to be a declining public interest in the issues. Once again, this appears to be a world-wide trend of which New Zealand is a part.

Like most societies today, New Zealand stands at a confused crossroads, unsure of which way to go. Ultimately, for lasting, constructive change in New Zealand, real leadership – and mentorship – is essential at all levels of life. It is not that the wisdom and inspiration are not here; they are all around us, but are often marginalised. As Bruce Lyons writes in *Standing for the Sacred*, we have forgotten what is sacred. We have forgotten too what communities actually are. We cannot look wistfully back to the past and neither should we. But there is no reason why anyone living in this country should be without hope and without a future. There is so much here for everyone that we could even provide some illumination for an overcrowded and troubled world.

To find a way, we need to recognise and value what we do have and to teach younger generations to be more confident and discriminating about what messages in bottles to take heed of. For a start, we might adopt respect for biodiversity as a principle of social as well as natural life. And we need to learn that compassion, that great quality of human nature and practice, need not be confined in its focus to the human race.

David Young

Mt Tasman and the Main Divide, Westland and Aoraki/Mount Cook National Parks

Tangata whenua at a celebration of Tongariro National Park's World Heritage status, Whakapapa, Central North Island

Interior, Manatuke Marae, Gisborne

Heni Sunderland, Manatuke Marae, Gisborne

15

ABOVE: Lake Waikareiti, Te Urewera National Park
LEFT: Beech trees in mist, Panekiri Bluff, Te Urewera National Park

Julia Taiapa, longtime resident of Hicks Bay, East Cape

Horsemen, Tolaga Bay, East Coast

ABOVE: Ratana church, Raetihi
RIGHT: East Island near East Cape, the most easterly point of mainland New Zealand

Phil in his self-built winery, Gisborne

Pine logging north of Whatatutu, East Coast hill country

Sunset over Gisborne and Poverty Bay

Surfing at Mount Maunganui, Tauranga

ABOVE: Leigh, surf shop, Gisborne
LEFT: Grace and Ayden at a cafe, Gisborne

Art student, Tairawhiti Polytechnic, Gisborne

A morning catch of hapuku, Hicks Bay, East Cape

Cleaning fresh hapuku, Hicks Bay, East Cape

ABOVE: Fumeroles in the central crater of White Island, Bay of Plenty
LEFT: Evening light on Mt Taranaki, Egmont National Park

Corn field, Wairoa, northern Hawkes Bay

Logging truck, Central North Island

Fishing competition, Tatapouri, near Gisborne

Father, son and dog at surfing competition, Makorori, near Gisborne

ABOVE: Mt Ngauruhoe from the summit of Mt Tongariro, Tongariro National Park
RIGHT: Waipunga Falls, Napier Taupo highway

Fishing for trout at Waitahanui, Lake Taupo

Mt Taranaki, seen from the beach at Mokau, north of New Plymouth

Jill and her horse, Tolaga Bay, East Coast

Tolaga Bay wharf, East Coast

Homestead at Muriwai, Poverty Bay

Girders of the Mohaka River railway viaduct, northern Hawkes Bay

Farmland near Tiniroto, inland from Gisborne

Sheep station north of Tolaga Bay, East Coast

Cattle droving on State Highway 2 between Gisborne and Opotiki

Sheep sale at the Gisborne stock yards

ABOVE: Narrow gorge in the Whirinaki River, Whirinaki Forest, Central North Island
LEFT: Ancient beech-podocarp forest, Whirinaki Forest, Central North Island

Beach near Devonport, looking towards Rangitoto Island, Auckland

Bride outside St Stephen's Chapel, Parnell, Auckland

Central Auckland and the Skytower, from the Waitemata Harbour

ABOVE: Outdoor cafe, central Auckland
RIGHT: Cafe waitress, Auckland

Participants at Pasifika, Auckland's annual Polynesian festival

Performer at Pasifika, Auckland

ABOVE: Cape Reinga lighthouse, at the northern tip of New Zealand
LEFT: Aerial view of downtown Auckland and the Skytower

Waiting backstage before performing at Pasifika

Handcrafts, Pasifika

Illuminated Skytower, seen from Ponsonby Road, Auckland

Stella walking past the Masonic Lodge, Warkworth, north of Auckland

ABOVE: Volcanic cliffs north of Piha, Auckland's west coast
LEFT: The shifting sands of Te Paki, 90 Mile Beach, Northland

Kauri forest, Trounson Kauri Park, Northland

Boulders and pohutukawa trees, Little Barrier Island, Hauraki Gulf

Selling fish at the Saturday market, Avondale, Auckland

On the wharf at Paihia, Bay of Islands

Repainting the 4 Square store, Russell, Bay of Islands

Heading seaward, Bay of Islands

Sculpture detail, Civic Square, Wellington

Te Papa, Museum of New Zealand, Wellington

Inner harbour and central Wellington, seen from Mt Victoria

Businessman, downtown Wellington

Eccentric motorcyclist, Wellington

Canoeing the Whanganui River, upriver from Pipiriki

School girls on an outdoor education course, Whanganui River

Sunrise at Civic Square, Wellington

Local iwi performing at Wellington's biannual International Festival of the Arts

ABOVE: Street performance, International Festival of the Arts, Wellington
LEFT: Sunset over Kapiti Island, on the Kapiti Coast north of Wellington

Ratana Church at Ratana, south of Wanganui

Suburban house, Wanganui

ABOVE: Main street, Carterton, Wairarapa
RIGHT: Cabbage trees in the wind, Wairarapa

Cape Terawhiti, the southwest tip of the North Island on Cook Strait

Shipwreck at Tora, north of Cape Palliser, southern Wairarapa coast

Castle Point lighthouse, Wairarapa coast

Windsheared kanuka, Wairarapa hill country

ABOVE: Dusky dolphins, Kaikoura
LEFT: Sunrise on railway lines, Mangamaunu, Kaikoura

Sperm whale on the surface, Kaikoura

Sawcut Gorge in the Waima River, Marlborough

The outer Marlborough Sounds, seen from Mt Stokes

Mum and Dad on the Cook Strait ferry

ABOVE: Mountain hut, Mt Robert skifield, Nelson Lakes National Park
LEFT: West Sabine River winding through beech forest, Nelson Lakes National Park

Wind and spring blossom, Port Hills, Nelson

Stone sculpture symposium, Nelson

Ladies amongst the cardigans, Nelson Agricultural and Pastoral Show

Primary school, Nelson

Christine, ceramic artist, Nelson

Jens and his granddaughter, Nelson

Tug of war, Nelson

On the road to a New Year festival, Nelson

ABOVE: Playing in the outgoing tide, Totaranui, Abel Tasman National Park
RIGHT: Sand patterns, Awaroa, Abel Tasman National Park

Shearers and their rouseabouts, Golden Bay

Mustering sheep near Farewell Spit, Golden Bay

Takaka Agricultural and Pastoral Show, Golden Bay

Cows returning to the paddock after morning milking, Golden Bay

Pilot whale stranding, Golden Bay

Mailboat near D'Urville Island, Marlborough Sounds

New Zealand Wearable Art Awards, Nelson

Super 12 rugby match, Nelson

ABOVE: Limestone arch near Karamea, West Coast
RIGHT: Rainforest at Ship Creek, South Westland

ABOVE: Rainbow over La Perouse, Cook River, Westland National Park
RIGHT: Evening light on the Southern Alps, Westland National Park

Farmhouse beneath the Brunner Range, West Coast

Bill at Okarito Lagoon, South Westland

ABOVE: Kahikatea forest, Lake Wahapo, Westland National Park
LEFT: Blowhole at the Pancake Rocks, Punakaiki, Paparoa National Park

ABOVE: Lake Matheson, Westland National Park
RIGHT: Remnant kahikatea near Fox Glacier, with Aoraki/Mt Cook and Mt Tasman behind

Horses, Karamea, West Coast

Dairy farmer at Karamea, West Coast

ABOVE: Climbers near the summit of Mt Tasman, Westland and Aoraki/Mount Cook National Parks
RIGHT: Middle reaches of the Franz Josef Glacier, Westland National Park

Rainy day at the corner dairy, Westport, West Coast

128

Wet day in the Grey Valley, West Coast

Japanese tourists pose in Cathedral Square, Christchurch

Robert McDougall Art Gallery, Christchurch

ABOVE: Road above Lyttelton Harbour, Banks Peninsula
LEFT: Interior of the Provincial Council Chambers, Christchurch

ABOVE: Hagley Park, central Christchurch
LEFT: Macrocarpa shelter belt, North Canterbury

Nor'west arch, Canterbury Plains

Heavy frost on farmland, North Canterbury

Thermal pools, Maruia Springs, Lewis Pass

Lake Tekapo and the Two Thumb Range, Mackenzie Country

Snowfall near Fairlie, South Canterbury

Poplar trees, South Canterbury

ABOVE: Hopkins Valley and the Dasler Pinnacles, Mackenzie Country
RIGHT: Country road near Lake Tekapo, Mackenzie Country

Nor'west clouds over Lake Pukaki and Aoraki/Mt Cook

Lake Pukaki and the Mackenzie Country from the summit of Aoraki/Mt Cook

Looking from the Eyre Mountains toward the Remarkables, near Queenstown

Farmgate near Tarras, looking toward the St Bathans Range, Central Otago

ABOVE: Subalpine beech forest, Milford Track, Fiordland National Park
RIGHT: Mackay Falls, Milford Track, Fiordland National Park

ABOVE: Breaksea Sound, Fiordland National Park
LEFT: Gales sweep Solander Island, Foveaux Strait

Stormy weather on Milford Sound, with Mitre Peak behind

Jetboating on the Shotover River, Queenstown

Red deer at Walter Peak, Lake Wakatipu

Tourists and paragliding above Queenstown

Bungy jumper, Queenstown

Reflections in the base lodge window, Coronet Peak Ski Area, Queenstown

Evening on the Queenstown foreshore

ABOVE: Sunset, Mt Aspiring, Mount Aspiring National Park
RIGHT: Schist tors, Old Man Range, Central Otago

Statue of Robbie Burns, Octagon, Dunedin

Ten Commandments, Five Rivers, Southland

Sheep amongst the swedes, Southland

Bayview Hotel, Bluff

Winter snow near Queenstown

Tussock country near Lake Onslow, Central Otago

Hills above the Cardrona Valley, Central Otago

Yellow-eyed penguins, Otago Peninsula

Granite tor, southern Stewart Island

Road on Pitt Island, Chatham Islands